"Psychologist Singer has written an accessible ... ...ctory general guide for caregivers of chronically ill children.... Reassuring and helpful, this small volume is a first step for parents of newly diagnosed children, one of few such titles.... Recommended."

-- Library Journal


"Alesia Barrett Singer has given an easily read first step for parents who are embarking on the difficult voyage of caring for a child with chronic illness. A must read for troubled parents. Her 'over the backyard fence' approach to an often overlooked problem provides an effective first step guide to help parents and families cope with chronic illness."

-- Praim S. Singh, M.S.W.
Executive Director
Rehabilitation Institute of Southern California


"Alesia Barrett Singer has provided invaluable information in a concise and easily understood format for parents of chronically ill children and/or professionals who work with this population. Her wide-ranging knowledge of health and psychology, family relationships, and children's development is conveyed to the reader in a warm and compassionate voice, with plenty of practical advice and referrals for further reading. Her book could be distributed in clinics, doctors' offices, support groups, or other intervention programs. An excellent addition to the literature for parents and professionals alike!"

-- Mindy S. Rosenberg, Ph.D.
Private Practice, Sausalito, California
Clinical/Community Psychologist;
Visiting Assistant Professor of Psychology
University of California, Berkeley

"It was truly a pleasure to read *Coping with Your Child's Chronic Illness*. This is a wonderfully succinct summary of the issues that are critical for parents to deal with if they wish to be effective parents after their child has been diagnosed with a chronic illness. My twenty-two years of pediatric practice have shown me that this is a very difficult and delicate subject, and the tone of your book, which is very 'communal,' will give the parents an understanding that they are not alone in their feelings and problems."

-- Mark S. Reuben, M.D., F.A.A.P.
Reading Pediatrics
Wyomissing, Pennsylvania


"I found this book to be comprehensive in its approach, sensitive to the needs of parents and children alike, spiced with humor (which helped keep the topic in perspective), as well as being the only book which clearly, in a straight-forward manner, assists a parent to be what they were created to be—their child's natural advocate. Often in a health care system strained by the mere numbers of its members, parents are looked upon as "junior partners" in the area of their child's care. Not so in *Coping With Your Child's Chronic Illness*."

-- Lynnie Morgan, Founder/Director
Mitochondrial Disorders Foundation of America
Concord, California

# Coping With

# Your Child's

## Chronic Illness

by Alesia T. Barrett Singer, M.A.

 Robert D. Reed Publishers
San Francisco, California

**Robert D. Reed Publishers**
750 La Playa, Suite 647
San Francisco, CA 94121
(650) 994-6570 • Fax: (650) 994-6579
E-mail address: 4bobreed@msn.com
Website: www.rdrpublishers.com

Editor and Typesetter: **Pamela D. Jacobs, M.A.**
Illustrations by **Bob Censoni**
Dover Publications, New York • Dover Clip Art Series
Cover Design: **Julia A. Gaskill**

---

Library of Congress Cataloging-in-Publication Data

Barrett Singer, Alesia T.
　　　Coping with your child's chronic illness / by Alesia T. Barrett Singer.
　　　　　　p.　cm.
　　　Includes bibliographical references.
　　　**ISBN 1-885003-14-5**
　　　1. Chronic diseases in children--Psychological aspects. 2. Chronically ill children--Family relationships. 3. Parents of handicapped children. I. Title.
RJ380.B37　1999　　　　　　　　　96-36373
618.92--dc20　　　　　　　　　　　　CIP

Manufactured, Typeset and Printed in the United States

*For my parents*

# Acknowledgments

A special thank you to my husband, Andrew Singer, and to my family for their years of love and unwavering support in all that I do.

Many thanks to Dr. Mindy Rosenberg, Jennifer Treuting, and Richard Renfro for their invaluable support and constructive editing. Thank you to everyone whose thoughtful comments went into the final manuscript. Additional thanks to Robert D. Reed and Pamela D. Jacobs for their support in publishing this book.

Originally I began working on this book for my Ph.D. program in the Psychology Department at the University of California at Berkeley. I would like to acknowledge the generous support provided to me during that time by the William F. and Albertine C. Cordes Scholarship and the Mentored Research Award from the University of California at Berkeley.

# Contents

1. Finding Out Your Child Has a Chronic Illness .... 1

2. Educating Yourself .............................................. 8

3. Becoming an "Advocate" .................................. 19

4. Communicating with Your Child ...................... 31

5. Potential Areas of Family Stress Associated
   with Having a Chronically Ill Child .................. 57

6. Concluding Thoughts ...................................... 65

   References ........................................................ 67

# Note To Readers

This book is sold with the understanding that the subject matter covered herein is of a general nature and does not constitute medical, legal, or other professional advice for any specific individual or situation. Readers who are planning to take action in any of the areas that this book describes should, of course, seek professional advice from their doctors, health care specialists, and other advisers, as would be prudent and advisable under their given circumstances.

# Chapter 1 –
# Finding Out Your Child
# Has a Chronic Illness

Most parents feel overwhelmed with conflicting emotions and thoughts when they hear that their child has a condition which will require regular medical treatment. It is important that you recognize that this is natural and try to allow yourself to have these thoughts and feelings without judging them.

Different parents have different ways of coping with finding out that their child has a chronic condition. Some parents react with their emotional side and need time to process their reactions and feelings emotionally. Other parents react with their intellectual side and gather as much information as they can to help them process what is going on with their child. Still other parents become overwhelmed and unable to do anything for a while until they can react to the diagnosis. No one way of coping is necessarily better than another.

Some important things to remember are:

☆ Recognize and accept your way of
   coping as what you need to do to help

you take care of yourself, your child, and your family.

&#9734; Make conscious efforts to turn to your friends and family to help you to cope in whatever way you need. Social support is invaluable in getting all of us through potentially difficult times.

&#9734; Plan for the future, but try to take things one day at a time. Especially if your child has a progressive condition, it can be overwhelming to think of your child's prognosis as a whole. By facing one day at a time, you can feel more in control of each new day.

&#9734; Expect that it will probably be a while before things have settled down and you are able to move ahead to become more active in finding out how you can help your child.

Dr. Elisabeth Kübler-Ross, a renowned doctor and researcher, described five stages of grieving (1969) which have been used as one way to explore and explain the responses and coping processes that parents, as well as chronically ill children, often experience. These five stages include:

1.   Denial
2.   Anger
3.   Bargaining
4.   Depression
5.   Acceptance

You may experience more than one stage at a time, such as feeling both angry and depressed about your child's diagnosis. You may not experience the stages in this order or even experience all of the stages. You also may pass through the stages more than once. Often times, parents pass through the various stages in a continuous, cyclical manner.

## Denial and Shock

We all like to believe that we are immortal, that nothing bad can happen to us. Even when parents feel "prepared" to hear that their child has a medical condition, the diagnosis almost always comes as a shock and brings feelings of disbelief.

Initial feelings of shock and disbelief are often mixed with or followed by feelings such as grief, helplessness, anger, guilt, despair, vulnerability, and frustration. Like denial, shock allows you to keep from being immobilized by overwhelming emotions. It is only when shock turns into pervasive denial that it becomes a problem.

## Anger

Because a child's diagnosis can make parents feel helpless, many parents of chronically ill children feel

some degree of anger toward "fate" or God for choosing their child. Having a child who is chronically ill means that you will have to make certain changes in your lives. Even what might seem to be small changes can be quite stressful. Parents commonly feel additional resentment and anger about the lack of available support and appropriate services. These feelings are frequently mixed with even more tormenting feelings of not being able to help your child, of not being able to "make it all better."

Unlike many other feelings, we often feel that it is not okay to be angry or to express anger, and that somehow anger cancels feelings of love. Anger, however, is not the opposite of love—indifference is. Anger in a family often results from intense feelings of caring and frustration when we can't help someone we love. It is important, however, to learn to manage and communicate angry feelings in healthy ways so that we do not hurt those we care about.

# Bargaining

Oftentimes the discovery of a child's illness presents a philosophical or religious crisis for parents. Many parents bargain with professionals and/or God in an attempt to restore their child's perfect health. They hope that if only they do all the "right" things from here on out, or if their child simply has the "right" medical treatment, everything will be as it was.

# Depression

Parents are responsible for their children's well being. Consequently, when a child becomes sick, parents often feel guilty. They feel that somehow they could have prevented their child's condition, that somehow they are to blame for their child being sick. These feelings easily lead to feelings of depression—feelings of sadness, lack of energy, and unhappiness in life.

In most cases, there is nothing you could have done to prevent your child from having become sick. Even in those cases where there are things parents might have been able to do to help prevent their child's illness, it is important for all parents to move on and do all they can for their child and family in the present without becoming "stuck" dwelling on the past.

Parents also become easily overwhelmed when the cost of regular medical treatments is a financial burden or when caring for their child requires that they make lifestyle changes. Although you might think something like rearranging your schedule to take your child to the doctor is a relatively small change, if it interferes with your regular schedule, it might be more stressful than you anticipated. Often, active planning of how to cope with the new changes in your life will help increase your feeling of being in control and lessen the likelihood that you will become overwhelmed.

Although it is important to allow yourself to feel whatever emotions you might be feeling, it is also important to seek help and support from family, friends, or professionals if your feelings begin to get in the way of your being able to take care of yourself or your child. (For more information about depression, please see "Potential Areas of Family Stress," Chapter 5.)

## Acceptance

Accepting that one's child has a chronic illness is the final stage of coping. However, this does not mean that the feelings and issues you have experienced in earlier stages will not come up again. It means that you have come to terms with the fact that your child has a chronic illness and can (at least for now) find out more about what you can do to help your child, your family, and yourself.

Accepting that your child has a chronic illness can be a very difficult thing to do. Once parents accept their child's condition, they are generally left with the question, "Okay, what now?" This book is designed to help you with some of the answers to that question.

## Notes

# Chapter 2 –
# Educating Yourself

Most parents are frightened when they hear that their child has a condition which will require regular medical treatment. The important thing is that when you are ready, you move beyond your fear and do not allow it to keep you from finding out all you can about your child's condition and how you can help him or her. The more you educate yourself, the more in control of your child's care you will feel.

As a parent of a child with a chronic illness, you will need to educate yourself about the following:

1. Facts concerning your child's illness
2. Facts about the treatments your child will require and the medications your child is or will be taking
3. Resources in your area for children, parents, and families

Although these may seem to be daunting tasks, they are important ones and may take less time to research than you think! Remember, depending on how you cope, it may be a while before you feel ready to take on these tasks. The important thing is that you take things at your own pace so you don't become overwhelmed.

Before you begin, purchase a notebook or staple some paper together so you can have a place to write down your questions and what you learn.

## Facts concerning your child's illness and medications

The following are resources you can turn to in order to gather more information about your child's condition:

1. Your child's doctor
2. Your pharmacist (if your child needs to take medication)
3. The library
4. A bookstore
5. Computer resources
6. Parent and nonprofit support groups

## Your Child's Doctor

The best place to start learning about your child's condition and any treatments and medications he or she might need is with your child's doctor or pediatrician. Although it might feel uncomfortable to ask questions of your child's doctor, your child's physician is probably the best person to answer some very important questions for you.

While it is important that you respect your doctor's expertise, you have a right to ask questions and to be given a complete and thorough explanation about your child's condition.

The following are some things you might want to discuss with your child's doctor:

☆ What condition your child has.

☆ What kinds of treatment are available.

☆ What medical treatment your doctor suggests.

☆ What the expected course of the illness is.

☆ How you can help lessen your child's symptoms.

☆ What impact your child's condition might have on your child and your family.

If you don't usually ask your child's doctor questions and the list above seems like a lot of questions to ask, try asking just one question at a time.

You do want to make sure that you understand the doctor's instructions regarding any medical treatment or monitoring your child will require. Especially with medications, you will want to make sure you understand the following:

✯ How much and how often you are supposed to give your child his or her medicine.

✯ What time of day you are supposed to give the medication.

✯ Whether the medication should be given before or after eating, or taken with food. Whether there are any foods that should not be taken with the medication (such as milk).

✯ What you should do if you forget to give your child his or her medication on time.

✯ What possible side effects there might be for the medicine your child needs to take.

✯ What other medications and substances you should avoid giving your child.

Most of all, ask questions and ask for clarification when you do not understand what the doctor is telling you. (For hints on how to remember all those questions you had, see "Becoming an Advocate," Chapter 3).

If you weren't able to get the answers you needed from your child's doctor, or you feel too uncomfortable to ask, don't fret—there are other places you can find answers!

## Your Pharmacist

Your neighborhood drug store pharmacist may be a less intimidating person than your doctor to talk to about any medications your child might need to take. Your pharmacist can address the issues listed above and can also give you the product information pamphlet provided by the drug manufacturer for the particular medication your child needs. Many pharmacies are also now providing customers with printouts from a company called Medi-Span, Inc. which list how to use the medication, cautions to consider with the medication, and possible side effects of which you should be aware. Ask your pharmacist if they have this information available.

## The Library

Many large hospitals have a health education library available for patient use. Find out if your hospital or HMO has one available and what types of information they carry that might be useful for you. You can also find a great deal of information at your local public library. The encyclopedia is a pretty good place to look for concise and clear information. Your library should have a current set of encyclopedias in the reference section.

You can also look up your child's illness in the card catalogue or on the library computer to find any books related to your child's illness. Depending on how common an illness it is, you should be able to find a handful of related books and may even find a book or two written by parents whose children have the same condition. Why not make an outing out of it—your child will probably enjoy finding some new books to read, and you can educate yourself at the same time.

For the adventuresome and those eager to learn more, you can generally find computer databases of current information on your child's condition and treatment options at any major university library. The reference librarian should be able to help you learn to use these databases in about five to ten minutes. These databases are generally known by the names:  Psych-Lit or Psych-Info for psychological literature on the impact an illness has on a child and family as well as how you can help your child comply with any medical treatment needed; and Medline for medical information on the condition and its treatment. Generally, the abstract (summary of the article) that is provided by the database will direct you to the articles you might find most helpful. Overview articles tend to summarize the findings across many research projects and can be a useful means of gaining a clearer picture of what is known about your child's condition.

# A Bookstore

Most of the major book stores now have extensive health sections where you can find current medical reference books, as well as a host of other books related to health. If you are looking for particular information, often the easiest way is to look up the topic in the index of the book to see whether it is covered. It is generally difficult to tell from the title or cover whether the book has information that would be helpful for you, so count on spending a little time browsing through the books.

# Computer Resources

There is a wealth of information currently available on CD-ROMs (computer software that comes on a compact disk) or through the Internet. If you have access to a computer with a CD-ROM drive, there are a number of health references available at most major computer stores. CD-ROMs can offer information ranging from basic anatomy and disease processes to comprehensive guides for medical services.

The Internet is a good resource for up-to-date information regarding illness, treatment, medications, relevant research, and support. If you have access to a computer and a modem, you can access the Internet through any number of on-line services, such as America Online (1-800-827-6364) or CompuServe (1-800-848-8199). Most Internet services offer a free trial membership, after which you pay a monthly service fee for a set number of hours of access time and hourly rates for any time beyond your limit.

You can often access the information you need more quickly and efficiently through the Internet than by going to the library or bookstore. For example, America Online has Health Channel (keyword: health) for discussion groups related to health concerns; Better Health (keyword: better health) for support groups, medical research information, and other medical references; Health Zone (keyword: health zone) for nutrition and fitness information and support; and Health Reference (keyword: health reference) for access to references such as MedLine, the Consumer Reports Complete Drug Reference, and the Merriam-Webster Medical Dictionary. Similarly, CompuServe gives you access to current medical research, and has a large online support network for people suffering from or caring for those suffering from chronic illness.

## Parent and Nonprofit Support Groups

Parent and nonprofit support groups can be a wonderful source of encouragement and information. Look into what support groups are available in your area. If you are unable to find a group that is specific to your child's illness, consider a support group for parents whose children have a range of illnesses. You will still be able to learn from and share in each other's experiences.

# Resources for Children, Parents, and Families

It is also important that you get to know what programs are available in your area to help your child, you, and your family cope with your child's chronic illness. Although you may never need to make use of the services they offer, it is useful to know where to find help in times of crisis.

There are a range of services available for individuals and families depending on your child's particular condition and how it is affecting your family. Resources come in many forms to suit the varying needs of different individuals and are offered both privately and through organizations. The following are some of the options which may be available to you:

* ☆ Support groups for parents, children, and siblings of chronically ill children to help in dealing with a variety of issues related to chronic illness.

* ☆ Educational meetings for people seeking to learn more about their child's illness, treatment options, and current research.

* ☆ A range of psychotherapy services for those who prefer or need individual help are generally available in each community. Many community based programs offer reduced fees.

- ✯ "Sick child care" centers where you can take your child when your child is unable to go to school and you cannot stay at home with him or her.

- ✯ "Respite care" where someone takes care of your child for a few hours so you can take a break.

- ✯ At home nursing help for administering treatment to your child.

Resources can be difficult to find. However, if you stick with it, you should be able to connect with the services you need or think you might need in the future. Your family doctor should be able to tell you the names of some programs that offer services in your area and most hospitals have a social services department which can offer referrals if necessary. Another place you can call for referrals is community mental health clinics which generally carry resource information for the county in which they are located. The Yellow Pages of your local telephone book is also a good place to look for referrals.

Educating yourself about your child's illness and about resources available to you is an important part of actively coping with having a chronically ill child. Although educating yourself takes time, it makes you better able to take care of the special needs of your child and family.

In addition, knowledge about your child's condition and treatment will make you a better "advocate" and communicator, which are the topics of the following two chapters.

Note: For a wonderful, comprehensive book containing a wealth of ideas, references, and resources, please read *500 Tips For Coping With Chronic Illness* by Pamela D. Jacobs, M.A. (Robert D. Reed Publishers, 1997). To order the book, you may use the order form in the back of this book or see the website: www.rdrpublishers.com.

## Internet Websites That May Be Useful:

- Healthfinder (www.healthfinder.gov/)
- American Medical Association (www.ama-assn.org/)
- Mayo Clinic (www.mayo.ivi.com/)
- MedWeb (www.gen.emory.edu/MEDWEB/medweb.html/)
- U.S. National Library of Medicine (www.nlm.nih.gov/)
- The Centers for Disease Control and Prevention (www.cdc.gov/)
- National Institutes of Health (www.nih.gov/) or (www.cc.nih.gov/)
- Columbia/HCA Healthcare (www.columbia-hca.com/)
- Federal Drug Administration (www.fda.gov/)
- Healthtouch (www.healthtouch.com/)
- Medscape (www.medscape.com/)
- MedicineNet (www.medicinenet.com/)
- American Academy of Pediatrics (www.aap.org/)
- KidsHealth (www.kidshealth.org/)

# Chapter 3 –
# Becoming An "Advocate"

One of the most difficult steps for parents after coping with the initial diagnosis is becoming an "advocate" for their child, their family, and themselves. Being an advocate for one's child is something that is familiar to all of us. It is like sticking up for your child on the playground when other children are being unkind. When parents have a child who is chronically ill, however, it requires them to become advocates for their child in ways that are often new to them. For example, most people are taught from an early age to respect professionals. Few people, however, are taught how to become active partners with professionals in the treatment of their children. Becoming an advocate is an ongoing process and one which most people have to work on for a long time before it is a comfortable role for them.

Four basic areas in which you can become an advocate:

1. Becoming an advocate for your child's physical health

2. Becoming an advocate for your child's emotional health

3. Becoming an advocate for your family's needs

4. Becoming an advocate for your own needs

Of course there are other areas in which you can become an advocate, but working on these is generally a good place to start.

## Becoming an Advocate for Your Child's Physical Health

Being an advocate for your child's physical health means learning to be an active partner with your child's doctor. Different people have different degrees of comfort in talking with physicians. Although it may be either difficult or easy for you, most people find that they forget some of the questions they wanted to ask their doctor, or forget what the answers were when they actually speak with their child's physician. The following are some methods you might find helpful in speaking with your child's doctor:

&#9734; Write down any questions you have and take them with you when you go to the doctor's office.

&#9734; Buy yourself a small notebook or take some paper and a pencil or pen with you so you can write down the information your doctor shares with you.

✺ Although it can be difficult, ask your child's doctor to explain things to you when you don't understand what he or she is telling you. Doctors often forget that they use technical words which are generally unfamiliar to most people.

✺ Try to be as open as you can with your child's doctor about your concerns—whether they are financial, emotional, medical, or otherwise, they are important for your doctor to understand so that he or she can help develop a practical medical treatment plan for your child. If your doctor suggests a medication that costs more than you can afford, it won't be an effective treatment.

✺ Find out who you can call in an emergency and whether your child should wear a medical bracelet to notify others of his or her condition in case of an emergency.

# Becoming an Advocate for Your Child's Emotional Health

In addition to being an advocate for your child's physical health, it is important to be an advocate for your child's mental health as well. When children are different from other children, they can be subject to prejudice, misunderstanding, and teasing by people who do not understand their differences. Chapter 4, "Communicating with Your Child" offers helpful tips on talking with your child which is an important part of becoming an advocate for your child. While you cannot anticipate all the potential misunderstandings, the following are some things you may want to keep in mind:

✴ It is important to talk with your child regularly about his or her feelings and what your child's concerns are regarding his or her illness and treatment. (For more on this, see Chapter 4.)

✴ It is also important to check in regularly with your child about how things are going at school and with peers. Problems in these areas can lead to difficulties with school work, low self-esteem, and psychological distress.

✮ Children can often be very cruel to other children who are in any way different. It is important for you to recognize this potential and prepare your child to cope with teasing. Talk with your child about how other children are often afraid of things they do not understand and make fun of children who are different. Help your child to think of things he or she can say in response to teasing. For example, even the phrase, "All kids have different things they are good at and different things that are harder for them" can be a helpful come-back. A child who feels empowered to deal with teasing and is prepared with a good set of come-backs is much less likely to feel victimized than a child caught off guard.

✮ Talk with your child's teacher and school nurse about any special needs your child has and what they should do in case of an emergency. By talking with them, you can feel assured that your child will be taken care of, and your child can be assured that everyone knows what to do if anything were to happen to him or her.

✮ In addition, talk with your child's teacher about your child's concerns. People often do not think about the consequences of discussing a child's illness, limitations, or treatment in front of other children. It can be very helpful to emphasize to your child's teacher how crucial it is that he or she not mention these issues in front of the other children in the classroom or on the playground.

✫ If your child's illness is physically apparent or keeps your child from being able to participate fully in activities with other children, talk with your child about whether he or she wants you to go and talk with the other children in his or her class. Oftentimes a discussion with your child's class about how your child may in some ways be different from them, but in all the important ways is just the same can be very helpful. In addition, a brief, simple explanation about your child's condition can also help the other children to understand what previously they might have feared simply because it was unfamiliar to them.

✫ Chronic illness is difficult for children as well as for parents. Children may communicate frustration and anger in ways that you might not recognize, but that look like misbehavior. If you notice changes in your child's behavior, think about what he or she might be trying to communicate and speak with your child about what is troubling him or her.

# Becoming an Advocate for Your Family's Needs

Becoming an advocate for your family means actively watching out for and anticipating the needs of your family. Chronic illness in any family can cause stress and cause attention to be focused on the child's illness. Therefore, attention may be taken away from other members of the family and from the family as a unit. Although the needs of your chronically ill child often seem more pressing, it is vitally important that the needs of each family member are recognized and met as best as possible. There are many ways to be an advocate for your family. Here are just a few:

✯ If your child requires intensive treatment, find ways to make the treatment part of a routine. When things become routine, they require less energy to be spent figuring out when it is scheduled, who is responsible, etc. and allow more time to be spent on other things like family.

✯ Schedule time for all family members to "check in" with each other about how they are feeling, what has been on their minds, and what they have been doing. Dinner together is a good time for this, but if your family schedules don't allow you to gather together at dinner time, try to find another time when you can all get together.

⭐ Take time out as a family to allow all of you to "escape" for some quality time together. It does not have to cost money to be enjoyable; you could go for a walk in the park together.

⭐ Encourage family members to talk openly and constructively about their fears, concerns, hopes, and emotions regarding your child's condition. Make sure that you try to keep family members from blaming the child for his or her illness.

⭐ Recognize that often so much attention and energy is focused on the chronically ill child that other family members can feel left out. Actively think about how you can reorganize your schedule so you can spend time with your other children and with your spouse or partner.

⭐ Healthy siblings may express their need for attention from you by misbehaving. It is important that you think about whether your healthy child's disruptive behavior is actually a call for much needed attention and respond accordingly. Even thirty minutes spent with each child can be incredibly effective in helping your healthy children feel cared for and special.

# Becoming an Advocate for Yourself

Learning to be an advocate for yourself is sometimes the hardest thing for a parent to learn. However, it is very important for you to look out for your own needs as well as the needs of your children. The unique challenges of having a chronically ill family member can create enormous stress for parents. It is extremely important for parents of chronically ill children to acknowledge this added stress and to actively pur-  sue some time for themselves. Parents with a chronically ill child are much more likely to "burn out" because of the extra time and effort required in caring for their child. Consequently, you need to learn how to protect yourself from burning out. Different people have different strategies. What's important is not what you do, but that it works for you.

Although you may feel too busy to take time out for yourself, or feel guilty about doing so, it's really important that you learn to set aside some time for yourself. Think of it as recharging yourself for your other obligations—if you let your battery run down, you wouldn't be able to be effective anyway!

Remember—it's essential that you take some time out for yourself!

Some strategies others have found to be helpful are:

✷ Allow yourself some "private time" to take a hot bath, or do something else that you find relaxing.

✷ When someone asks you to do them a favor, say you'll think about it and get back to them. This will allow yourself time to decide if you're really up to taking on another commitment.

✷ Run errands together with friends so you get to visit with friends and accomplish some necessary errands as well.

✷ Find someone to take care of your child or children for the evening so you can go out with your spouse, partner or friends.

✷ Take time out regularly to exercise—it can actually boost your energy level, lift your spirits, and help you to feel more positively about yourself.

- ☆ Create your own support group. Ask several friends to help support you and your family on an ongoing basis. Keep them in touch with your struggles and needs and ask if they can help support you by doing things such as baby-sitting or cooking dinner once a month.

- ☆ Try to keep a sense of humor and perspective about daily hassles. Remind yourself about what is really important to you and try to focus your energy on those things.

- ☆ Talk about your feelings and frustrations as they arise. By talking openly about what is bothering you, you help keep the lesser stresses from building up and weighing you down.

- ☆ Know your limits. Set realistic and flexible goals. Think about what tasks during your day are essential and do those things first. Reward yourself for the things you get accomplished and do not punish yourself for those you did not get around to accomplishing.

- ☆ Create your own support group. Ask several friends to help support you and your family on an ongoing basis. Keep them in touch with your struggles and needs. Ask if they can help support you by doing things such as baby-sitting or cooking dinner once a month.

✭ Try to keep a sense of humor and perspective about daily hassles. Remind yourself about what is really important to you and try to focus your energy on those things.

✭ Talk about your feelings and frustrations as they arise. By talking openly about what is bothering you, you help keep the lesser stresses from building up and weighing you down.

✭ Know your limits. Set realistic goals. Think about what tasks during your day are essential and do those things first. Reward yourself for the things you get accomplished and do not punish yourself for those you did not get around to accomplishing.

Learning to become an advocate for your child, your family, and yourself is a continual process. It will probably be easier for you to be an advocate for your chronically ill child than for your other children, your marital or partner relationship, or yourself. It is important, however, that you remember that your healthy children and your marriage or partner relationship need your attention as well. Lastly, don't forget to take care of yourself. You can't take care of the rest of your family if you are burned-out.

# Chapter 4 – Communicating with Your Child

Speaking with your child about his or her medical condition and what chronic illness means for your child's life is incredibly important. However, most parents find it uncomfortable and difficult to talk with their child about the illness. Although discussions of this type usually get easier with practice, the following information may help your discussions go a bit more smoothly.

This chapter will try to answer the following questions:

1. Why is it important that I speak with my child about his or her illness?
2. Why is it so hard to talk with my child about these things?
3. How can I talk with my child about his or her condition?
4. Why do I need to make this a part of our ongoing conversations?
5. What kind of information should I share with my child at different ages or developmental levels?
6. Are there particular times when I should be more aware of the need to talk with my child?

# Why is it important that I speak with my child about his or her illness?

As adults, we often forget the creative and rich fantasy life of children. Children are always trying to make sense of their world, and if they lack clear information about the cause and treatment of their condition, even very young children will create their own explanations for why they have a chronic illness. These explanations are almost always born out of a child's fears that he or she is somehow to blame for his or her illness, or that he or she deserves to be sick for doing something bad and is now being punished, or that he or she became ill because of a personal inadequacy. Additionally, some children may fear that their chronic medical condition makes them "weird" or unlikable by other children. Others may fear that it means that they aren't "normal" or are "defective." Whatever your child's fears are, it is important that you talk with him or her about them. In talking with your child, you can help dispel some of the fears, share others, and perhaps most importantly, emphasize how important and special he or she is.

Even if you do communicate the facts to your child at a level you think he or she comprehends, children often understand things differently than we think they do. Children frequently turn facts into fears or fantastical notions that seem to have little or no connection to the original information they were given. All of this may make you think, "Why should we tell them anything then?" However, it is important to realize that it is always better to talk with your child about his or her illness. Speaking with your child gives you a chance to find out what your child understands about his or her condition as well as to dispel any fears or misconceptions he or she may have. By providing your child with clear, concise information and speaking with your child about his or her fears, you can help your child to feel less worried and more positive about himself or herself.

Speaking with your child about his or her condition also helps your child learn that it is okay and important to talk about his or her condition and how it is affecting him or her. By talking with your child and asking about things that he or she might wonder about or worry about, you help your child learn that it is normal to have such questions and concerns. In addition, you communicate that you are open to helping him or her find answers to the questions and that you want to help with his or her concerns.

## Why is it so hard to talk with my child about these things?

Talking with one's child about his or her medical condition can be a very difficult thing for parents to do.

There are generally four main concerns which get in the way of parents talking with their children:

1. Parents' own resistance to talking about their child's condition
2. Parents' concerns about the actual discussion
3. Lack of time
4. Resistance on the part of the child to talk about his/her illness and how it is affecting him/her

Oftentimes the biggest hurdle for parents in talking with their child is the feeling that somehow talking about their child's condition makes it more of a reality. By recognizing that it is important for them to discuss their child's illness with their child, parents have to admit that their child's condition is something which has an impact on their child's and their lives and that it isn't going to magically disappear if they don't talk about it. This can be a very difficult thing for parents to face, but it is essential that parents come to terms with the potential impact their child's condition has on their child and their family if they are going to be able to help their child, their family, and themselves. Avoiding talking with a child about his or her illness and its impact on his or her life communicates to the child that talking about these things is taboo and leaves the child to cope with his or her concerns and questions alone. While it may feel as if talking about your child's condition makes it more of a reality, your child needs you to help him or her talk about these things.

Secondly, most parents experience some degree of anxiety about sitting down and talking with their child about his or her illness. For some parents it is difficult because they worry that their child will think that they are focusing too much attention on his or her illness. For other parents, it is difficult because thinking and talking about their child's condition is very emotional for them and they themselves do not want to talk about it. For yet other parents, talking with their child about his or her illness is difficult because they worry about not being able to answer their child's questions and feel overwhelmed by difficult questions like, "Why me?" Other parents worry about how much information they should share with their child and how this information should be conveyed.

If you are able to figure out what is making you most anxious about the discussion, you can take steps to reduce that anxiety. Some things you might try to help you feel less anxious are:

⋆ Set time aside to think about what you want to cover in your discussion.

⋆ Write down a list of things you want to say.

⋆ Try role playing with a friend, your spouse or partner to help you feel more confident.

⭑ Tell yourself that you have to do this for your child and focus on why it is important.

⭑ Talk with friends about what they might say in your position.

Feeling like you do not have enough time is another potential obstacle to sitting down and speaking with your child about these matters. In fact, lack of time seems to be a frequent problem in our fast-paced lives. Nonetheless, making time to talk with your child about his or her illness is extremely important. Sometimes conversations about a child's illness arise spontaneously because the child voices concerns, asks questions, or seems distressed. Other times, however, it is important to schedule discussions into your busy life just as you would schedule any other kind of appointment.

Your child's resistance may be a fourth obstacle to a discussion about his or her illness. While children often say that everything is fine and that they don't need to talk, most are actually desperate to have answers to lingering questions and to be able to discuss their fears and fantasies. In addition, children often respond to stress with hyperactive behavior and may only be able to sit still for a few minutes of discussion at a time in the beginning. However, even if your child responds with, "Not this again," it is important for you to keep in mind how crucial it is to have ongoing conversations with your child about his or her illness and how it is affecting him or her. It also gives you a wonderful opportunity to emphasize your child's strengths and to emphasize what makes him or her so unique and special. Open communication between parents and children is a key ingredient in rearing a well adjusted child.

As discussed, there are any number of reasons why sitting down with your child and talking with him or her about his or her illness might feel like a daunting task. Understanding why it might feel difficult for you, setting aside time for you and your child to talk, and anticipating your child's concerns are important steps in helping you to feel more empowered to talk with your child. Eventually, however, you will need to simply give it a try. "How?" you ask? Read on...

## How can I talk with my child about his or her condition?

While no book can provide you with the exact answers to this question, this book will try to provide you with some helpful things to keep in mind.

The first step is really to "set the stage" for your discussion:

☆ Set aside enough time for you and your child to speak so that you do not have to prematurely end the conversation or rush the discussion. Some parents have found it helpful to talk in the car when they know they will be driving for longer periods of time. This can be helpful, especially in the beginning, because having your talk in the car makes the conversation seem less formal and because it's time when neither of you have other things to do.

☆ Second, even if you have scheduled a time to talk, don't try to have the discussion when you are upset, frustrated, tired, or otherwise "stressed out." Take a minute or two for yourself to see if you can gather yourself together. If you still feel in a negative mood, it is better to reschedule the discussion than to risk communicating negative feelings instead of openness and caring.

☆ Third, it is important that you be as comfortable as you can. Try to convey to your child that any questions or worries that he or she might have are important and that you are open to hearing and discussing them.

The second step is to have a plan about how you want to convey information and to encourage an active discussion between you and your child. In creating your plan, you should be realistic about what you think you can accomplish, think about how you might respond to sensitive issues, and recognize that your plan should be flexible to allow you to respond to your child's needs. Try not to feel like you need to accomplish everything in one discussion.

As for the actual discussion, the following tips should be of some help:

✳ You may want to begin by asking your child about what he or she already knows and understands about his or her illness, even if you think you know the answer. By finding out this information first, you can build upon what your child already knows, clarify information that has been misunderstood, and dispel false notions. By asking your child to tell you what he or she already knows, you also begin by engaging him or her in the conversation instead of setting up the discussion to seem like a lecture from you, the parent. You might want to ask questions such as: What do you think children with (your child's condition) are like? Do you know anyone else with (the same condition)? What do you think someone with (your child's condition) might be good at doing? What do you think he or she might have trouble doing? What do you think happens to children with (your child's condition) as they grow older? Are there things which are confusing to you about all of this?

✮ Try to remember to talk about issues in ways that are meaningful and understandable to your child. One way to do this is to use examples from your child's own experience and treatment in explaining things. Remember, your child is most likely going to understand information that is presented in a simple, clear, and concise manner.

✮ In explaining the cause for your child's illness, do not try to explain more than is necessary to answer your child's questions. You can always provide more complete information as your child grows. Always use language and comparisons that are familiar to your child. Also, refrain from using comparisons that might be frightening for children. For example, children are likely to be scared by examples of bacteria or viruses being like bugs running around in their bodies.

✮ Remember to focus on your child's experience of what it feels like to have a chronic illness. Ask your child about his or her worries and concerns. This may be the most important part of your conversations.

With younger children, statements that do not directly ask children about their own feelings, but that leave room for them to talk about what someone else with the same condition might feel are often useful in opening up the conversation. For example, you might say something like: "I wonder what a girl with (your child's condition) might worry about. I think maybe she might feel scared that something was wrong with her or worried that other children won't like her because they think she's different from them."

☆ Talk with your child about the benefits and limitations of his or her treatment. Help your child to understand that while medications can do their part, your child must also do his or her part. For example, you might say, "Your insulin shot helps your body to run smoothly, but it can't do it all on its own. You need to eat healthy foods too, to keep your body healthy." Help your child feel in control of and responsible for his or her own well being in ways that are appropriate under the circumstances. This could mean everything from emphasizing responsibility for home treatments and active cooperation in the treatment plan, to getting physical exercise according to your child's abilities.

☆ Make sure to spend some time talking with your child about how he or she feels about his or her treatment. In addition to listening to your child's feelings about his or her treatment, watch for feelings of concern that the treatment is burdensome on your family. Many parents in their attempt to make their children feel better about difficult or painful treatments minimize how difficult or painful they actually are for the child. Allow your child to talk about how difficult, painful, or bothersome his or her treatment or limitations are and empathize with his or her feelings. Even simply repeating what your child is saying can feel supportive to him or her. (For example, "It really hurts when the doctor has to draw all that blood.") Of course, if your child is becoming unnecessarily anxious about the treatment, after hearing his or her concerns, you would want to reassure your child that it is not as bad as he or she thinks. Then talk about ways to make it less anxiety-provoking for your child.

✯ Every step of the way, actively encourage your child to ask questions and participate in the discussion. Check in with your child about what he or she understands of what you are saying. Simply asking whether your child understands or not generally leads children to simply say "yes" regardless of whether they really understand. Instead, you might say, "I want to make sure I have been clear enough. Why don't you tell me in your own words what you understand of what

I've been saying." By doing this, you can clarify any misunderstandings or misconceptions that your child may have about what you have said.

☆ Give equal attention to recognizing how having a chronic illness can be very difficult for anyone and to recognizing your child's efforts. Also, accentuate the positives. Emphasize the positive areas in which your child excels and which make him or her special and unique. Discuss the things that your child can do despite his or her condition, and how he or she can safely participate in things that he or she enjoys.

## Why do I need to make this a part of our ongoing conversations?

Children need to be updated with new information at each stage in life. As children grow, their understanding of how the body works and the impact their illness has on their life changes. What a child understands at one age may become distorted or forgotten at another. Therefore, it is not enough to assume that the discussion you had with your child when you first explained his or her illness to him or her will carry your child through a lifetime. Instead, it is better to think of the need to have conversations with your child as an ongoing responsibility. By having periodic discussions with your child, you can remain in touch with your child's concerns about his or her condition, clarify misconceptions he or she might have, and build upon what he or she remembers from your last conversation. Most importantly, frequent conversations emphasize that you're concerned about how your child's condition is affecting him or her and communicate how important your child's feelings are to you.

## What kind of information should I share with my child at different ages or developmental levels?

It is important to provide developmentally appropriate information for children at different stages of their lives. While the following information does not provide the particulars for your discussions with your child, it does provide some guidelines to help you think about how to discuss your child's illness with him or her. Even if your child is older, it may be helpful for you to read the information for younger children because each step builds upon the last.

In addition, the age ranges given below are only guidelines. If your child is developmentally delayed, it will be important for you to adjust what you say accordingly. For example, if your child is 8 years old, but is developmentally closer to a 5 year old, use the information listed for children between the ages of 2 and 6 years old to help guide your discussions.

Remember, every discussion should emphasize that your child is a very special person and should recognize your child's efforts and strengths.

★ Children who are between the ages of 2 and 6 years old benefit most from very concrete, experiential explanations of illness. Young children do not yet understand more abstract, complicated notions of how their body functions and how internal body processes are related to illness. Rather, they understand illness in terms of external observable events like having symptoms such as a runny nose or having to visit the doctor. In speaking to your younger child, try to use specific examples of your child's symptoms or treatment instead of using generalizations to describe what it means to have his or her condition. Children at these ages are not cognitively ready for a complicated explanation about their condition. The focus for discussions with a young child should be that he or she is experiencing a few specific symptoms and that the doctor is helping you to make those symptoms better.

If your child is taking medication or has specific treatments, it is important that you discuss these as well even with very young children. Again, discussions about treatment should be concrete and focus on your child's experience. At this stage, a simple statement like, "The doctor has given us a special type of medicine that helps kids like you and will help you too," should be enough.

Lastly, because almost all childhood illnesses are contagious, children at this stage usually think that all illnesses and even broken bones are contagious and can be "caught." Consequently, it is important that you really explain that some illnesses can be caught but that other illnesses aren't the kind that can be caught. Depending on your child's condition, you may also want to explain that while some things like colds can be easily caught from friends, other illnesses are very difficult to catch. It may be helpful for you to discuss your child's condition as a problem that the doctor is helping to solve rather than an illness that the doctor is helping to treat.

With children this young, the goal is to let them know that you are concerned about their feelings, that you and the doctor are working to make things better, and that you want them to share their worries and concerns with you.

* <u>Children who are between the ages of 7 and 10 years old benefit most from concrete, organized explanations of illness.</u> Children at this stage still do not quite understand how internal body processes function and are related to illness. They understand illness best in terms of external observable events from their own experience rather than internal processes. Children at these ages are able, however, to remember more of what you discuss with them, and are beginning to understand logical relationships between things. For example, a child in this stage can generally understand that he or she has several specific, observable symptoms which are related to his or her condition which has a name. Furthermore, the same child could probably understand that because of these specific problems he or she has, he or she has to go to the doctor and have treatment to help with them.

At this stage, children are more able to use language to describe how they feel and how they interpret the things that happen to them. It is especially important, then, to talk with your child about how he or she feels about the illness and the things that are a part of the treatment plan. You can also use the information your child shares with you and your child's own words that he or she uses to talk about his or her experience to tailor your discussions with your child.

Children between these ages are also beginning to understand causal relationships. While their understanding generally remains limited in this area, you can begin to discuss that your child's condition is because his or her body (not internal systems) has a difficult time doing a particular thing which is related to one of your child's symptoms. For example, if your child has asthma, you might say, "When you feel like you're choking it is because sometimes your body has a difficult time getting enough air. This problem is called 'asthma.' Your inhaler helps your body get the air it needs."

If your child is taking medication or has specific treatments, it is important that you continue to discuss these as well. Again, discussions about treatment should be concrete and focus on your child's experience. At this stage, you can begin to discuss the fact that the particular treatment helps your child's body to do what it needs to do. Children at this stage can understand contradictions and can be told that while the treatment does its part, that they need to do their part as well for it to work.

Finally, children at this stage can often benefit from simple analogies, comparisons with things that are familiar to them, that help explain the child's condition. However, it is important that you remember several key issues when using analogies:

☆ Use simple analogies which are based on things familiar to your child, such as race cars or super-computers.

☆ Pay attention to how your child might misinterpret the analogy. For example, try to stay away from using comparisons with broken or damaged objects.

☆ Put your analogy in a positive light to enhance your child's self esteem. For example, if your child has diabetes you might say, "You are like a super race car that needs a very special oil to run properly. If the race car didn't have its special oil, it would have trouble running smoothly."

☆ Include treatment issues in your analogy (such as the oil/insulin in the previous example).

☆ Let your child participate in developing the analogy. For example, you could ask what else might help the race car run smoothly (good fuel/food).

☆ Explain to your child the connection between his or her condition and the analogy you use. For example you might say, "Your body is like the race car, and your insulin is like the special oil. Just as the race car needs the special oil to run smoothly, your body needs your insulin to run smoothly."

☆ Ask your child to explain the analogy back to you so that you can correct any misinterpretations.

With children at this stage, the goal should be to clarify information they already have, update them with new age-appropriate information, find out about and address their worries and concerns, and maintain open communication.

☆ <u>Children who are around 11 years old and older benefit most from more complex explanations of illness which explain the entire illness process</u>. The major change for children in this stage is that they can understand more fully the relationship between the underlying cause of their condition, their symptoms, and their how different systems in the body work to maintain health and how when certain systems are not working properly, people get sick. Discussions with children around 11 years old and older, then, can contain explanations of the actual physiological processes involved in their condition. Discussions with older children should also begin to include explanations of the psychological role involved in health and illness. For example, such discussions could be about how stress can worsen existing symptoms.

Younger children at this stage can begin to understand generalizations about their symptoms and their condition, and can understand ideas about things which are not directly observable. As a consequence, discussions about symptoms and treatment should include information about both the concrete symptom or treatment and your child's internal or psychological experience of it. In addition, the analogies you used at earlier stages can be developed in greater detail or replaced with more fitting and complex analogies.

At this stage, the focus of the discussions should be on answering your child's questions, providing your child with more complete information, emphasizing the importance of your child's role in his or her health, and addressing concerns

which arise as your child enters into adolescence
and peer relationships take on greater importance
in his or her life.


## Are there particular times when I should be more aware of the need to talk with my child?

Times of transition are usually the times when children
need updating the most. Check in with your child
periodically about his or her worries. In talking with
your child about his or her concerns as they arise, you
can try to stay ahead of the game before the concerns
lead to anxiety and depression. Some periods of
transition to keep in mind are:

✻ <u>Entry into school</u>. Entry into school is anxiety
   provoking for many children and can be much
   more so for children with chronic illnesses. When
   children enter school, the
   security and safety of
   home is lost and new
   pressures of achieve-
   ment and peer relationships are added. Addi-
   tionally, parents' own
   anxiety around this
   transition can contrib-
   ute to children's anxiety.

To help yourself feel more comfortable with your child's entry into school, address your concerns. If you are worried about who will be able to take care of your child if the need arises at school, meet with the school nurse and your child's teacher to discuss what measures should be taken if your child needs medical attention at school. You should provide the school with all pertinent emergency information for your child.

In addition, entering into school can be especially difficult for chronically ill children because of the potential for other children to tease them. Oftentimes peers can be very hurtful in their teasing. If your child takes medication, cannot participate in certain activities, or is otherwise different from the other children, take time to help him or her understand why other children tease. Teach him or her empowering statements to say in response to other children's teasing. A good come-back is always helpful in keeping your child from feeling victimized. Most importantly, talk with your child about how much it hurts when other children tease him or her.

It may also be important to impress upon your child's teacher how important it is to your child's self esteem that he or she refrain from mentioning your child's illness, limitations, or medication needs in front of the other children. Furthermore, you may want to discuss what concerns and worries your child has about attending school so that the teacher can be more sensitive to these issues. If your child has a noticeable disability, it may be important for you to visit your child's classroom and talk with the other students about what it means for your child to have a chronic illness. You can talk with them about the fact that while in some ways it means he or she is different, that in all the important ways your child is just like the rest of the students.

✻ <u>Changing schools</u>. Changing schools in many ways presents the same stress as first entering school. There are new teachers, new academic pressures, and new peer relationship anxieties. Talk with your child about what it is like for him or her to be going to a new school. Find out what he or she likes about the new school as well as what he or she does not like about it. Ask your child what worries him or her about the transition.

✻ <u>Developmental changes: puberty</u>. Puberty is a difficult time for many children because their bodies are going through many changes for which they may not be prepared. Puberty for any child is an important time for open communication between parents and children. For children with chronic illnesses, it is a time of increased anxiety about their development in light of their illness, about how their illness may make them feel different from other children, and about how their illness will affect their potential for intimate relationships.

✵ Developmental changes: adolescence and young adulthood. As children become adolescents and young adults, friendships, peer groups, and dating relationships take on increasing significance. Adolescence is a crucial time to check in with children about issues of self esteem (how they feel about themselves and their abilities), relationships with friends and partners, and concerns about how their illness might influence these areas.

Adolescence is also a time when chronically ill children often begin to resist taking their medication or following through with their treatment plan because it increases their feeling of being different from their peers. It is important to discuss these issues when they first arise. By listening to your adolescent's reasons for not wanting to take his or her medication or follow through with his or her treatment plan, and by empathizing with him or her, you may be able to avoid a drawn-out struggle over treatment issues. It will be important for you to help your adolescent understand that although he or she may not want to follow through with the treatment plan, it is extremely important for your adolescent's health that he or she does.

Make your adolescent feel increasingly in charge of and responsible for his or her well being instead of you being in charge of the treatment regimen.

Although it may be a difficult thing for you to do, talking with your child on a regular basis about his or her illness and how it is affecting him or her is perhaps the most important thing you can do to help your child cope with his or her condition. Remember: face your own resistance to and anxieties about talking with your child, plan what you want to discuss, set a special time aside for your discussion, and recognize that it may be difficult for your child to learn to talk about his or her condition as well. With practice, this difficult process will only get easier!

## Notes

# Chapter 5 – Potential Areas of Family Stress Associated with Having a Chronically Ill Child

Families with a chronically ill child must cope with problems generally far more complex than other families. It is important that you are aware of the potential areas of stress for your family. Although different family circumstances will create different stresses for each family, there are potential pitfalls of which every family should be aware.

⭐ <u>Parent Burn-out</u>: While all parents need periodic respite from their roles as caretakers, parents of chronically ill children need this respite even more. Parents of ill children often put aside their own needs for the sake of their children. While this may be effective in the short term, over time it puts parents at risk for burning out. It is important that you recognize your own need for respite and pursue it for your own sake, as well as your children's sake. Burned-out parents are ineffective parents.

✭ <u>Family Disequilibrium or Imbalance</u>: Families with a chronically ill child must often spend disproportionate amounts of time and resources attending to the needs of the chronically ill child. In families with more than one child, this can mean that the needs of healthy siblings risk being unmet. The challenge is to maintain a sense of family balance in spite of the increased needs of your chronically ill child.

Frequently, other siblings can feel left-out or ignored when all of the family's energies seem to be focused on the chronically ill sibling. It is extremely important that you not allow yourself to fall into a pattern of putting aside the needs of your other children for the needs of your chronically ill child. Sometimes it is hard to remember that your children who are well need your caring and attention as much as your child who is ill.

*Even eating an ice cream together can be a special time of sharing.*

However, it is essential that you spend time with them too. If you find yourself spending more time with your child who is ill than your healthy children, schedule regular times that are set aside for you to spend with each of your other children. A half hour spent together can have a powerful effect on your healthy child and on you and your family. Spending time with your other children helps them to feel that their needs are important in spite of the pressing needs of their sibling, helps you to not develop feelings of guilt for spending all of your time attending to the needs of your chronically ill child, and helps chronically ill children not develop feelings of guilt about consuming all of your energy such that their siblings suffer as a result. All your children need some quality time with you to feel that they are special, cared for, supported, and loved.

Marital or partner imbalance can also result from the increased demands on parents' time or differences in the way parents respond to their child's illness. When one or both parents' time is consumed with attending to their child's special needs, the marital or partner relationship can often suffer. It is important to recognize the needs of the couple relationship in  spite of the pressing needs of the child. By finding time to attend to each other's needs, you will feel more replenished and able to deal with your family's needs.

In addition, oftentimes parents or partners respond very differently to having a chronically ill child. Be aware that you and your spouse or partner may have very different coping strategies. It is important to recognize your differences and respect each other's way of coping. If one of you needs to talk a lot about your feelings and the other cannot listen because it makes him or her feel more overwhelmed, it is important for the person who needs to talk to find friends or a support group with whom to talk.

☆ <u>Parent Fear and Worry</u>: Parents of chronically ill children suffer from far greater fear and worry

about their child than parents of healthy children. This increase in fear and worry about their child can lead to feelings of chronic fatigue and depression. Therefore, parents need to find ways to talk about, address, and alleviate some of their worries by going to counseling or attending a support group.

☆ <u>Depression in Parents and Children</u>: Chronic illness can increase the risk of developing depression in parents, chronically ill children, and otherwise healthy siblings. The increase in stress and worry as well as a lowered sense of competence in many parents of chronically ill children often leads to feelings of depression in parents. For chronically ill children, feelings of vulnerability, anxiety about the future, and of being different from other children can often lead to feelings of depression as well. Impaired mobility and stressful treatment procedures increase a chronically ill child's risk for becoming depressed. For siblings of ill children, depression can result from feelings of not being taken care of when it seems as if all the parents' time and efforts are focused on caring for the ill sibling.

Talking with your child about how he or she is feeling, and watching for major changes in your child's activity level, sleeping patterns, friendships, eating habits, and school performance can help you determine whether your child is feeling depressed. Changes toward either too much or too little of a particular activity should serve as warning signs that your child might be depressed. For example, some signs of depression are: eating too much or having no appetite, sleeping many hours and feeling lethargic or being hyperactive and irritable, spending

an unusual amount of time at home alone, or staying out more than usual. It is very common for younger children to report increases in stomach aches or to misbehave and become unmanageable when they are feeling depressed.

It is important that you find resources in your area such as therapy, counseling, or support groups to help you, your child, or other members of your family cope with depression. You should seek professional help if you find that nearly every day for two weeks or more that your child or anyone in your family is feeling depressed or hopeless or no longer feels interested in his or her usual activities, and is experiencing some of the following symptoms:

* Significant change in appetite
* Significant change in sleeping patterns
* Uncharacteristic restlessness or sluggish- ness
* Lack of energy
* Feelings of worthlessness, self-reproach, or inappropriate guilt
* Diminished ability to concentrate
* Recurrent thoughts about death or suicide

If your child makes any comments about wanting to die or discusses suicide in any form, take these comments seriously even if he or she reassures you otherwise. Your child's thoughts about suicide or harming him or herself should <u>always</u> be taken seriously. If your child makes any such comments, seek help immediately.

☆ <u>Overprotection of the Chronically Ill Child</u>: Because parents of chronically ill children worry much more about their ill child's well being, they often restrict their child's independence and overprotect him or her in ways which aren't good for their child's development. Some of the most important tasks of childhood are emotional maturation, separation, and individuation. In order for your child to be able to master these developmental steps, he or she needs to be allowed the opportunity to gain increasing independence. While this may be very difficult for many parents, it is important that chronically ill children are given as much freedom as is appropriate. If you are concerned about whether you are overprotective of your child, or if other people have told you that you shelter your child, seek assistance from others to help you learn what is an appropriate amount of independence for your child.

☆ <u>Conflict Between Dependence and Autonomy</u>: One of the main tasks of childhood is to develop autonomy or independence. However, given the special treatment needs of many chronically ill children and given the increase in parental anxiety about their child's well being, developing autonomy from parents can be a very conflictual task for chronically ill children. Allowing a chron-ically ill child to become autonomous can be difficult for parents. Struggles between parental desire for control and a chronically ill child's desire for independence often center around treatment issues. These struggles, however, can have potentially serious consequences and should be addressed immediately. While parents need to think creatively about how their child can feel more in control of his or her treatment, children also need to understand the potential health consequences for not adhering to treatment.

If you think you, your child, or your family is struggling with any of the above issues or other stresses which you feel you cannot deal with on your own, seek help. While it may feel difficult to turn to others for help, no one can cope with stress alone. Social support and outside resources can offer you or your family added assistance when necessary. It is always better to find help when the problems begin than to wait until they have become unmanageable for you.

# Chapter 6 –
# Concluding Thoughts

Families with chronically ill children often have to face many difficult challenges. It is my sincere hope that this book will be a helpful resource for you and your family in learning to talk about, live with, and cope with chronic illness.

*Alesia T. Barrett Singer*

# Notes

# References

Altman, D., & Revenson, T. (1985). Children's understanding of health and illness concepts: A preventive health perspective. Journal of Primary Prevention, 60, 53-67.

American Psychiatric Association. (1994). Diagnostic and statistical manual of mental disorders. Fourth edition. Washington, DC: American Psychiatric Association.

Anderson, B., & Coyne, J. (1993). Family context and compliance behavior in chronically ill children. In N. Krasnegor, L. Epstein, S. Bennet Johnson, & S. Yaffe (Eds.), Developmental aspects of health compliance behavior (pp. 77-89). Hillsdale, NJ: Lawrence Erlbaum Associates, Inc.

Band, E., & Weisz, J. (1990). Developmental differences in primary and secondary control coping and adjustment to juvenile diabetes. Journal of Clinical Child Psychology, 19, 150-158.

Berry, S., Hayford, J., Ross, C., Pachman, L., & Lavigne, J. (1993). Conceptions of illness by children with juvenile rheumatoid arthritis: A cognitive developmental approach. Journal of Pediatric Psychology, 18, 83-87.

Bibace, R., & Walsh, M. (1980). Development of children's conceptions of illness. Pediatrics, 66, 912-917.

Bibace, R., & Walsh, M. (1981). Children's conceptions of illness. In R. Bibace & M. Walsh (Eds.), New directions for child development: Children's conceptions of health, illness, and bodily functions (pp. 31-48). San Francisco, CA: Jossey Bass.

Billings, A., Moos, R., Miller, J. J., & Gottlieb, J. (1987). Psychosocial adaptation in juvenile rheumatic disease: A controlled evaluation. Health Psychology, 6, 343-359.

Bird, J. E., & Podmore, V. (1990). Children's understanding of health and illness. Psychology and Health, 4, 175-185.

Bobrow, E., AvRuskin, T., & Siller, J. (1985). Mother-daughter interactions and adherence to diabetes regimens. Diabetes Care, 8, 146-151.

Cole, R., & Reiss, D. (Eds.). (1993). How do families cope with chronic illness? Hillsdale, NJ: Lawrence Erlbaum Associates, Inc.

Cosper, M., & Ericson, M. (1985). The psychological, social, and medical needs of lower socioeconomic status mothers of asthmatic children. Journal of Asthma, 22, 145-148.

Daniels, D., Miller, J., Billings, A., & Moos, R. (1986). Psychosocial functioning of siblings of children with rheumatic disease. Journal of Pediatrics, 109, 379-383.

Davis, P., & May, J. (1991). Involving fathers in early intervention and family support programs: Issues and strategies. Children's Health Care, 20, 87-92.

Dimigen, G., & Ferguson, K. (1993). An investigation into the relationship of children's cognitive development and of their concepts of illness. Psychologia, 36, 97-102.

Dura, J., & Kiecolt-Glaser, J. (1991). Family transitions, stress, and health. In P. Cowan & M. Hetherington (Eds.), Family transitions (pp. 59-76). Hillsdale, NJ: Lawrence Erlbaum Associates.

Hymovich, D., & Dillon-Baker, C. (1985). The needs, concerns, and coping of parents of children with cystic fibrosis. Family Relations, 34, 91-97.

Jacobs, P. (1997). 500 Tips For Coping With Chronic Illness. San Francisco: Robert D. Reed Publishers.

Kashyap, L. (1981). The family's adjustment to their hearing-impaired child. The Indian Journal of Social Work, 47, 31-37.

Kazak, A. (1989). Families of chronically ill children: A systems and social-ecological model of adaptation and challenge. Journal of Consulting and Clinical Psychology, 57, 25-30.

Kerns, R., & Curley, A. (1985). A biopsychosocial approach to illness and the family: Neurological diseases across the lifespan. In D. C. Turk, & R. D. Kerns (Eds.), Health, illness, and families: A lifespan perspective (pp. 146-182). New York: Wiley.

King, K., & Hanson, V. (1986). Psychosocial aspects of juvenile rheumatoid arthritis. Pediatric Clinics of North America, 33, 1221-1237.

Kübler-Ross, E. (1969). On death and dying. New York: Macmillan.

Kübler-Ross, E. (1981). Living with death and dying. New York: Macmillan.

Luterman, D. (1987). Deafness in the family. Boston: Little, Brown and Company.

Milavic, G. (1985). Do chronically ill and handicapped children become depressed? Developmental Medicine and Child Neurology, 27, 677-682.

Perrin, E., & Gerrity, P. S. (1981). There's a demon in your belly: Children's understanding of illness. Pediatrics, 67, 841-849.

Perrin, J. (1985). Chronically ill children in America. Caring, 4, 16-22.

Potter, P., & Roberts, M. (1984). Children's perceptions of chronic illness: The roles of disease symptoms, cognitive development, and information. Journal of Pediatric Psychology, 9, 13-25.

Roberts, M., Koocher, G., Routh, D., & Willis, D. (Eds.). (1993). Readings in pediatric psychology. New York, NY: Plenum Press.

Sargent, J. (1983). The sick child: Family complications. Journal of Developmental and Behavioral Pediatrics, 4, 50-56.

Treuting, J. (1995). Talking with your kid about ADD. Unpublished manuscript. University of California, Berkeley, Psychology Department.

Whitt, K., Weiss, D., & Taylor, C. (1979). Children's conceptions of illness and cognitive development. Clinical Pediatrics, 18, 327-339.

# About the Author

**Alesia T. Barrett Singer, M.A.** is a doctoral candidate in clinical psychology at the University of California at Berkeley, where she earned an M.A. in psychology. She received her B.A. in psychology from Yale University.

During the past decade, she has focused much of her studies and research on the special challenges and experiences of chronically ill children. She has worked with many different populations, including deaf children, children with autism, children with learning disabilities, and children with pervasive developmental disorders. Although her current research focuses on the unique experiences of siblings in a family, she maintains her interest in assessment and intervention with special needs populations.

She and her husband, Andrew Singer, enjoy traveling, scuba diving, and spending time outdoors with their two dogs.

# Books Available From Robert D. Reed Publishers:

| Book Title | Each | Qty. | Sub-Total |
|---|---|---|---|
| *House Calls: How we can all heal the world one visit at a time* by Patch Adams, M.D. | $11.95 | ___ | ___ |
| *500 Tips For Coping With Chronic Illness* by Pamela D. Jacobs, M.A. | 11.95 | ___ | ___ |
| *Coping With Your Child's Chronic Illness* by Alesia T. Barrett Singer, M.A. | 9.95 | ___ | ___ |
| *New Low Fat This For That* by Meryl Nelson | 7.95 | ___ | ___ |
| *Celebration of Spirit* by Kathy Safranek | 9.95 | ___ | ___ |
| *Live To Be 100+* by Richard G. Deeb | 11.95 | ___ | ___ |
| *Healing Is Remembering Who You Are* by Marilyn Gordon (hypnotherapist) | 11.95 | ___ | ___ |
| *Lovers & Survivors: A Partner's Guide To Living With & Loving A Sexual Abuse Survivor* by S.Y. de Beixedon, Ph.D. | 14.95 | ___ | ___ |
| *Super Kids In 30 Minutes A Day* by Karen U. Kwiatkowski, M.S., M.A. | 9.95 | ___ | ___ |
| *50 Things You Can Do About Guns* by James M. Murray | 7.95 | ___ | ___ |
| *Get Out Of Your Thinking Box* by Lindsay Collier | 7.95 | ___ | ___ |
| *The Funeral Book* by Clarence W. Miller | 7.95 | ___ | ___ |
| *Not Over My Dead Body: The Truth About Organ Donation* by Clarence W. Miller | 5.95 | ___ | ___ |

Shipping & handling: $2.50 for first book; $1.00 for each additional book. California residents please add 8.5% sales tax. Discounts for large orders. Special offer: order any 3 books, get 4th book free! Total enclosed: $_____

**Send orders to or contact for more info. (manuscripts welcome):**
**Robert D. Reed Publishers**
750 La Playa St., Suite 647 • San Francisco, CA 94121
Phone: 650/994-6570 • Fax: 650/994-6579
Email: 4bobreed@msn.com • www.rdrpublishers.com

Please include payment with orders. Send indicated book/s to:

Name:_____

Address:_____

City:_____State:_____ Zip:_____

Phone:(____)_____Fax:_____E-mail:_____